Letts

KS2 Success

Age 7-11

English

Test

Practice Papers

Laura Griffiths and Shelley Welsh

Contents

Introduction and instructions **3**

Set A

English reading paper answer booklet **5**

English grammar, punctuation and spelling Paper 1: questions **20**

English grammar, punctuation and spelling Paper 2: spelling **34**

Set B

English reading paper answer booklet **37**

English grammar, punctuation and spelling Paper 1: questions **52**

English grammar, punctuation and spelling Paper 2: spelling **66**

English reading booklets **73**

Answers and mark scheme **93**

Spelling test administration **101**

(pull-out section at the back of the book)

Introduction and instructions

How these tests will help your child

This book is made up of two complete sets of practice test papers. Each set contains similar test papers to those that your child will take at the end of Year 6 in English reading and English grammar, punctuation and spelling. They can be used any time throughout the year to provide practice for the Key Stage 2 tests.

The results of both sets of papers will provide a good idea of the strengths and weaknesses of your child.

Administering the tests

- Provide your child with a quiet environment where they can complete each test undisturbed.
- Provide your child with a pen or pencil, ruler and eraser.
- The amount of time given for each test varies, so remind your child at the start of each one how long they have and give them access to a clock or watch.
- You should only read the instructions out to your child, not the actual questions.
- Although handwriting is not assessed, remind your child that their answers should be clear.

English reading

- Each test is made up of three different texts and an answer booklet.
- Answers are worth 1, 2 or 3 marks, with a total number of 50 marks for each test.
- Your child will have **one hour** to read the texts in the reading booklet and answer questions in the answer booklet.
- Some questions are multiple choice, some are short answers where only a word or phrase is required, and others are longer and followed by several lines on which to write the answer.
- Encourage your child to look at the mark scheme after each question to help them know how much detail is required in their answer.

English grammar, punctuation and spelling

Paper 1: questions

- Contains 50 questions, with each answer worth 1 mark.
- Your child will have **45 minutes** to complete the test paper.
- Some questions are multiple choice and may require a tick in the box next to the answer. Some require a word or phrase to be underlined or circled while others have a line or box for the answer. Some questions ask for missing punctuation marks to be inserted.

Paper 2: spelling

- Contains 20 spellings, with each spelling worth 1 mark.
- Your child will have approximately **15 minutes** to complete the test paper.
- Using the spelling test administration guide on pages 101–102, read each spelling and allow your child time to fill it in on their spelling paper.

Marking the practice test papers

The answers and mark scheme have been provided to enable you to check how your child has performed. Fill in the marks that your child achieved for each part of the tests.

Please note: these tests are **only a guide** to the level or mark your child can achieve and cannot guarantee the same level is achieved during the Key Stage 2 tests.

English reading

	Set A	Set B
English reading paper	/50	/50

These scores roughly correspond with these levels: up to 20 = well below required level; 21–30 = below required level; 31–40 = meets required level; 41–50 = exceeds required level.

English grammar, punctuation and spelling

	Set A	Set B
Paper 1: questions	/50	/50
Paper 2: spelling	/20	/20
Total	/70	/70

These scores roughly correspond with these levels: up to 24 = well below required level; 25–43 = below required level; 44–53 = meets required level; 54–70 = exceeds required level.

When an area of weakness has been identified, it is useful to go over these, and similar types of questions, with your child. Sometimes your child will be familiar with the subject matter but might not understand what the question is asking. This will become apparent when talking to your child.

Shared marking and target setting

Engaging your child in the marking process will help them to develop a greater understanding of the tests and, more importantly, provide them with some ownership of their learning. They will be able to see more clearly how and why certain areas have been identified for them to target for improvement.

Top tips for your child

Don't make silly mistakes. Make sure you emphasise to your child the importance of reading the question. Easy marks can be picked up by just doing as the question asks.

Make answers clearly legible. If your child has made a mistake, encourage them to put a cross through it and write the correct answer clearly next to it. Try to encourage your child to use an eraser as little as possible.

Don't panic! These practice test papers, and indeed the Key Stage 2 tests, are meant to provide a guide to the level a child has attained. They are not the be-all and end-all, as children are assessed regularly throughout the school year. Explain to your child that there is no need to worry if they cannot do a question – tell them to go on to the next question and come back to the problematic question later if they have time.

Key Stage 2

English reading

Reading answer booklet

Time:

You have **one hour** to read the texts in the reading booklet (pages 75–83) and answer the questions in this answer booklet.

Maximum mark	Actual mark
50	....

First name	
Last name	

Date of birth	Day		Month		Year	

> **Questions 1–16 are about *A Mad Tea Party* (see pages 76–77 in the reading booklet).**

1 Where is the scene set?

_____

1 mark

2 Why is Alice very small?

_____

1 mark

3 Look at the opening conversation.

Find and **copy** the clause Alice says just before she sits down at the table.

_____

1 mark

4 Which character offered Alice a drink?

Tick **one**.

the Hare ☐

the Hatter ☐

the Narrator ☐

the Dormouse ☐

1 mark

5 Use the following line to answer question 5.

Alice: *Then it wasn't very civil of you to offer it!*

What does the word *civil* mean in this line?

Tick one.

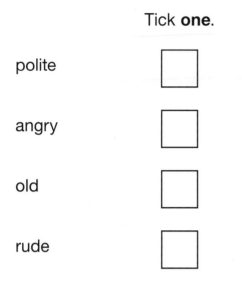

polite

angry

old

rude

6 Look at the Narrator's opening lines.

Identify **one** phrase that suggests Alice is correct in saying there is room for her to sit down.

_____

_____

7 Explain why Alice says, *'it's very rude!'*.

_____

_____

8 What stops the characters arguing?

_____

_____
1 mark

9 At the end of the passage the Narrator says, '*The conversation drops*'.

What does the word *drops* mean in this context?

_____
1 mark

10 After reading the text, how would you describe the character Alice?

_____

_____
1 mark

11 This text has been written as a play script.

Give **two** features of this genre that appear in the text.

1. _____

2. _____
1 mark

12 Look at the title of the extract: *A Mad Tea Party*.

Explain fully why this is an appropriate title, referring to the text in your answer.

_____

_____

_____

1 mark

13 **Find** and **copy one** stage direction from the text.

_____

1 mark

14 What is a synonym for the word *riddle*?

Tick **one**.

solution ☐

puzzle ☐

sentence ☐

argument ☐

1 mark

9

15 Explain the role of the Narrator in the play script.

_____

_____

16 Look at the title of the extract: **_A Mad Tea Party_**.

Which of the following would be the most suitable replacement for this title?

Tick one.

An Ordinary Tea Party ☐

An Unusual Tea Party ☐

A Boring Tea Party ☐

A Quiet Tea Party ☐

17 What is the name of the largest island of the Isles of Scilly?

_____

1 mark

18 *The Isles of Scilly are made up of five inhabited and approximately 140 other islands.*

What does the word *inhabited* mean?

Tick **one**.

deserted ☐

far away ☐

people live there ☐

tropical ☐

1 mark

19 Look at the paragraph beginning: *To reach the Isles of Scilly from the mainland . . .*

Give **two** ways visitors can reach the islands.

1. _____

2. _____

1 mark

11

20 Read the advantages and disadvantages of the two methods of transport. Which would you recommend for the following visitors? Give reasons for your answers **using the information in the text**.

A day visitor with no luggage: _____

_____

_____
1 mark

A family who are staying for a week who want to see dolphins swimming:

_____

_____

_____
1 mark

21 What does the word *common* mean in the sentence below?

There are many different types of birds on the islands, ranging from common birds such as sparrows, thrushes and gulls, to more unusual birds like puffins, cuckoos and wheatears.

_____

_____
1 mark

22 Would you like to visit the Isles of Scilly? Give **three** reasons for your view. Use the text to help you.

1. _____

2. _____

3. _____
1 mark

23 Compare how someone participating in and someone watching a gig race would be involved.

Participating: _____

_____

Watching: _____

_____

2 marks

24 This text was written to **inform** people about the Isles of Scilly.

Give **two** features of information writing that appear in the text.

- _____

- _____

2 marks

25 List **three** activities that the leaflet suggests for tourists to do when visiting the Isles of Scilly.

1. _____

2. _____

3. _____

1 mark

26 How do the locals usually travel around the islands? Give **two** modes of transport.

1. _____

2. _____

1 mark

27 In what format are you most likely to see this text?

Tick **one**.

a poster ☐

a travel leaflet ☐

a storybook ☐

a school magazine ☐

1 mark

28 When describing what tourists can see and do on the Isles of Scilly, the writer has deliberately chosen language that will have an effect on the reader.

Some of the words in the table below are underlined.

Explain the effect of these words in each sentence.

Language used	Explanation of the effect of the language
. . . *flock* to the island to race . . .	
. . . *waiting* to be explored . . .	
. . . *swirling golden* beaches . . .	

3 marks

29 What is the setting for the passage?

_____

30 Why did Joseph say, *'It's the whole world, this place is'*?

Tick **one**.

He thinks it's the best place to be. ☐

He doesn't know life anywhere else. ☐

31 *. . . Jim was looking up at the high walls that surrounded the workhouse, and at the bleak sky above it.*

Give **one** reason why the walls were high.

_____

32 Look at the paragraph that starts *It was impossible to tell . . .*

Explain how in this paragraph Jim realises he's been in the workhouse for a year.

_____

_____

_____

_____

33 *It was then that the little secret promise that had nestled inside him began to flutter into life like a wild thing.*

At this point in the story, what do you think Jim was thinking?
What was the *little secret promise*?

_____

_____

_____ 1 mark

34 *The teacher hauled him off his stool . . .*

Which word below is a synonym for the word *hauled*?

Tick one.

poked ☐

pushed ☐

persuaded ☐

pulled ☐

1 mark

35 Why did Jim say he didn't mind when Mr Barrack was beating him?

_____

_____ 1 mark

36 What reasons did Tip give for not going with Jim?

_____

_____
1 mark

37 _'A daft boy, you are,' said Tip._

Do you think Tip was correct to say this to Jim? Give examples from the text to support your answer.

_____

_____
1 mark

38 Describe the relationship between the two main characters, Jim and Tip, throughout the extract. Give examples from the text to support your answer.

_____

_____

_____

_____

_____
2 marks

39 Why did Jim say, '*Seems like I was born here*'?

_____

1 mark

40 Draw a line to match each event below to show the correct order from 1–6, as it appears in the extract.

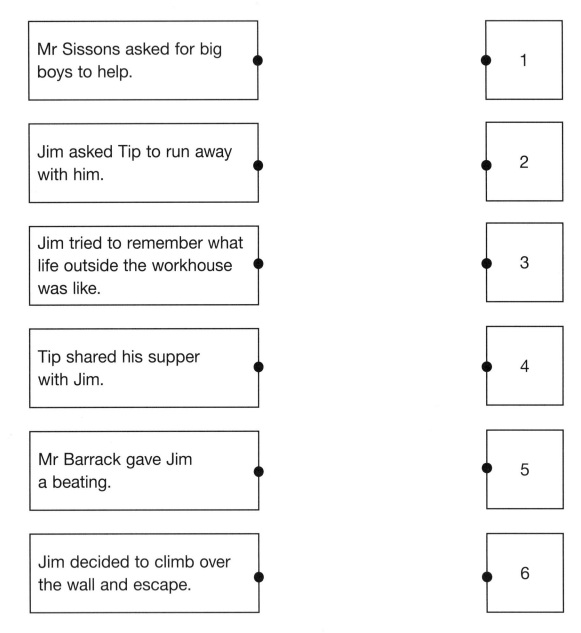

Mr Sissons asked for big boys to help.	1
Jim asked Tip to run away with him.	2
Jim tried to remember what life outside the workhouse was like.	3
Tip shared his supper with Jim.	4
Mr Barrack gave Jim a beating.	5
Jim decided to climb over the wall and escape.	6

1 mark

41 Find and copy **two** words which suggest Mr Barrack was pleased he had caught Jim talking.

Mr Barrack sprang down from his chair, his eyes alight with anger and joy. 'You spoke!' he said to Jim, triumphant. 'It was you.'

_____

_____ 1 mark

42 When describing Jim's feelings throughout the extract, the writer has deliberately chosen language that will have an effect on the reader.

Some of the words in the table below are underlined.

Explain the effect of these words in each sentence.

Language used	Explanation of the effect of the language
Jim's wild thoughts <u>drummed</u> inside him . . .	
. . . the <u>beating</u> inside him was like a wild bird now . . .	
. . . a shimmer of pain and <u>thrumming</u> wings.	

3 marks

SET
A

English
grammar,
punctuation
and spelling

PAPER 1

Key Stage 2

English grammar, punctuation and spelling

Paper 1: questions

Time:

You have **45 minutes** to complete this test paper.

Maximum mark	Actual mark
50	

First name	
Last name	

Date of birth	Day		Month		Year	

1 Tick the boxes where **determiners** have been used correctly.

Tick **two**.

an elephant ☐

an drum ☐

a octopus ☐

a superhero ☐

1 mark

2 Tick the word that means to find out.

Tick **one**.

choose ☐

discover ☐

invite ☐

repeat ☐

1 mark

3 Circle one verb in each underlined pair to complete the sentences using **Standard English**.

We **was / were** going to play outside on our bikes.

I **done / did** well in my maths test this morning.

1 mark

4   Add **inverted commas** to each direct speech below.

Wait for me! shouted Orla.

Ouch! My hand hurts.

Freddie whispered, Are you scared?

1 mark

5   Circle the **verb** in the sentence below.

Olivia and Sandip were building sandcastles at the beach.

1 mark

6   Which sentence shows the correct agreement between **subject** and **verb**?

Tick **one**.

The authors writed letters to the newspaper.

The authors wrote letters to the newspaper.

The authors write letter to the newspaper.

The authors writes letters to the newspaper.

1 mark

7   Add the missing **full stops** and **capital letters** to the sentence below.

nottingham is located in the east midlands the river that runs

through nottingham is called the river trent

1 mark

8 Circle the **conjunction** in the sentence below.

Since it was very cold outside, Sam decided to fasten his coat.

1 mark

9 Draw a line to match each **prefix** to the root word to make a new word.

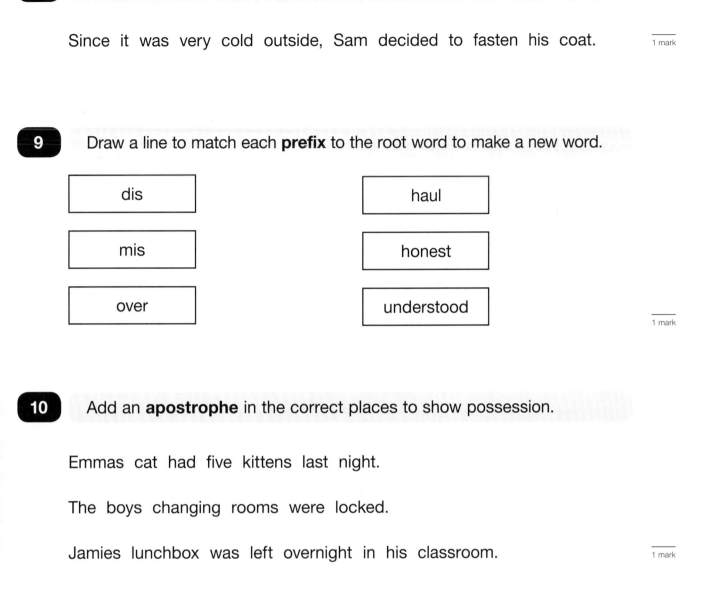

dis	haul
mis	honest
over	understood

1 mark

10 Add an **apostrophe** in the correct places to show possession.

Emmas cat had five kittens last night.

The boys changing rooms were locked.

Jamies lunchbox was left overnight in his classroom.

1 mark

11 Rewrite the sentence adding **two dashes** in the correct places.

William Shakespeare a famous author wrote the play 'Macbeth'.

_____

_____

1 mark

12 Underline the **main clause** in the sentence below.

Although she is younger than me, my sister is much taller.

1 mark

13 The incomplete sentences below are instructions in a recipe.
Add **two adverbials of time** to make the two sentences correct.
Remember to use correct punctuation.

_____ check you have the correct ingredients.

_____ turn the oven on to 180 degrees.

1 mark

14 Choose **one** of the **question tags** below to complete the sentence.

haven't you	haven't we	didn't you

You've been learning about materials in science, _____?

1 mark

15 Use the **past progressive** form of the verbs in the box to complete the sentence below.

to dance	to play

While the band _____, I _____ with my friends.

1 mark

16 Tick the option that correctly introduces the **subordinate clause** in the sentence below.

The teacher was pleased with the children's work, _____
he gave them extra playtime!

Tick **one**.

despite ☐

therefore ☐

however ☐

finally ☐

1 mark

17 Insert a **comma** in the correct place in the sentence below.

Feeling confident the pianist played to a room full of people.

1 mark

18 Circle the **adjective** in the sentence below.

Mum carefully topped the pudding with some whipped cream.

1 mark

19 In the sentence below, what **word class** is the word <u>they</u>? Put a tick next to your answer.

I wish they would be quiet now!

Tick **one**.

adjective ☐

preposition ☐

verb ☐

pronoun ☐

1 mark

20 Which of the events below is the **most likely** to happen?

Tick **one**.

I will wash the car today. ☐

I should go to work. ☐

I might watch a film. ☐

I could play in the garden. ☐

1 mark

21 Draw a line to match the words to the correct sentence type.

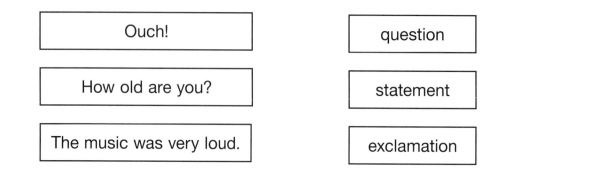

Ouch!	question
How old are you?	statement
The music was very loud.	exclamation

1 mark

22 Circle the most suitable **pronoun** to complete the sentence below.

he	his	it	me

Zane ate his dinner and then _____ went outside to play.

1 mark

23 Underline the **adverbial phrase** in the sentence below.

Later that evening, we said goodbye and began our journey home.

1 mark

24 Add **three commas** in the correct places in the sentence below.

Mangoes kiwis apples pineapples and strawberries are all types

of fruit.

1 mark

25 Write this sentence in the **past tense**.

We laugh at each other's funny jokes.

_____

1 mark

26 Circle the **conjunction** in the sentence below.

I am allowed to watch television while eating my dinner.

1 mark

27   Use the words below to complete the table.

ancient	new	small	large	wealthy	poor

	Synonym	**Antonym**
sad	unhappy	happy
rich		
big		
old		

28   Insert the missing **punctuation** in the sentence below.

The skateboard park located behind the playground is to be used

by children who are over eight

29   Rewrite the sentence below putting **ellipses** in the correct places.

On your marks ready steady go!

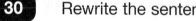

30   Rewrite the sentence below in the **active** voice.

The ancient ruins were visited by the historians.

31 Change the **nouns** to **verbs**.

Noun	Verb
simplification	to
calculation	to
magnification	to

1 mark

32 Circle the **preposition** in the sentence below.

The girl walked up the stairs.

1 mark

33 Rewrite the sentence below adding a **subordinate clause**.
Remember to use the correct punctuation.

The farmer went into his field.

_____

_____

_____

1 mark

34 Write out the words from the boxes below to make **one** sentence.
You can use the boxes in any order.
Remember to punctuate your answer correctly.

came to visit us		at Christmas

who lives in France		My uncle

_____

_____

1 mark

35 Underline the **relative clause** in the sentence below.

The old lady who was shouting at her neighbour was feeling angry.

1 mark

36 Write a suitable question to fit the answer below.
Remember to use the correct punctuation.

Question _____

Answer   He takes the bus.

1 mark

37 Circle the **two** words that show a **command** in the sentences below.

Put the flour and the butter in the bowl. Mix them together carefully.

1 mark

38 Write a **pronoun** in the space to make the sentence correct.

The boy ran up the school drive. _____ was late again!

1 mark

39 Complete the sentence below with a **contraction** that makes sense.

Why _____ you find your homework?

1 mark

40 Choose the correct form of the **past tense** of the verbs below to show a **continuous action**.

to dance

When I _____ in the show I

to smile

_____ all the time.

1 mark

41 Add **inverted commas** to punctuate the speech below.

What time does the train leave the station? Mary asked the guard.

Three minutes past ten, the guard answered.

1 mark

42 Where should a **question mark** be added to make the sentence below correct?

Tick **one**.

"Where are you going" the bus driver asked.

↑ ↑ ↑

☐ ☐ ☐

1 mark

43 Use the **co-ordinating conjunctions** in the box to correctly complete the sentence below.
Use each conjunction **once**.

or   but   and

The books _____ DVDs need returning to the library on

Monday _____ Tuesday _____ remember

it is closed each day for lunch.

1 mark

44 Rewrite the sentence below so that it starts with a **subordinate clause**. Remember to use a **comma** in the correct place.

I read a book while I was waiting to see the doctor.

_____

1 mark

45 Which of the sentences uses **dashes** correctly?

Tick **one**.

The cat – fast asleep – on the rug – was keeping warm by the fire. ☐

The cat – fast asleep on the rug – was keeping warm by the fire. ☐

The cat fast asleep, on the rug – was keeping warm – by the fire. ☐

The cat – fast asleep on the rug, – was keeping warm by the fire. ☐

1 mark

46 Underline the **fronted adverbial** in the sentence below.

With his sports kit on, Tom was ready for the game.

1 mark

47 Use the **subjunctive mood** to complete the sentence below so that it becomes more **formal**.

If the bus _____ late again, the children would be cross.

1 mark

48 Complete the table below by adding a **suffix** to each noun to make an **adjective**.

Noun	Adjective
child	
courage	
despair	
hope	
caution	

1 mark

49 What does the root <u>circ</u> mean in the word family below?

circumference   **circle**   **circumnavigate**

Tick **one**.

around   ☐

behind   ☐

above   ☐

below   ☐

1 mark

50 Circle one **verb** in each underlined pair to complete the sentences using **Standard English**.

I **went / goes** swimming at the weekend.

My friends Joe and Stella **was / were** there too.

1 mark

SET
A

English
grammar,
punctuation
and spelling

PAPER 2

Key Stage 2

English grammar, punctuation and spelling

Paper 2: spelling

You will need to ask someone to read the instructions and sentences to you. These can be found on page 101.

Time:

You have approximately **15 minutes** to complete this test paper.

Maximum mark	Actual mark
20	

First name	
Last name	

Date of birth	Day		Month		Year	

Spelling

1 Jai hurt his _____ playing tennis with his friends.

2 The _____ forecast for today is mostly sunny and warm.

3 Our _____ little kitten had scratched the carpet.

4 Mangoes, pineapples, kiwis and oranges are all types of _____.

5 We are going on a _____ hunt tomorrow.

6 The new clothes didn't fit so I need to _____ them to the shop.

7 My ambition is to play football for my _____.

8 The _____ was extremely busy this afternoon.

9 At break time, we play with the outdoor _____.

10 The _____ water boils at is 100 degrees Celsius.

11 The doctor said the rash was highly _____.

12 Sam won a _____ he entered at school.

13 Jemima was an _____ height for her age.

14 Our family eats _____ for breakfast.

15 The actress was very _____ on the stage.

16 The flowers in the bathroom are _____.

17 The weather is very _____ today.

18 There is a _____ coming from the large window.

19 The building must be evacuated _____ if the fire alarm rings.

20 The _____ members all attended a meeting at the school last night.

Key Stage 2

English reading

Reading answer booklet

Time:

You have **one hour** to read the texts in the reading booklet (pages 85–92) and answer the questions in this answer booklet.

Maximum mark	Actual mark
50	....

First name						
Last name						
Date of birth	Day		Month		Year	

1 Look at the sentence.

It felt soft and warm and slightly furry, like the skin of a baby mouse.

The sentence contains:

Tick **one**.

a metaphor ☐

a simile ☐

personification ☐

alliteration ☐

1 mark

2 *James stopped and stared at the speakers, his face white with horror. He started to stand up, but his knees were shaking so much he had to sit down again on the floor.*

Write how James is feeling.

_____

1 mark

3 *The creatures, some sitting on chairs, others reclining on a sofa, were all watching him intently.*

Which word is the correct synonym of *intently*?

Tick **one**.

casually ☐

closely ☐

quickly ☐

strangely ☐

4 Draw a line to match each creature to the description James gives when he **first** meets them.

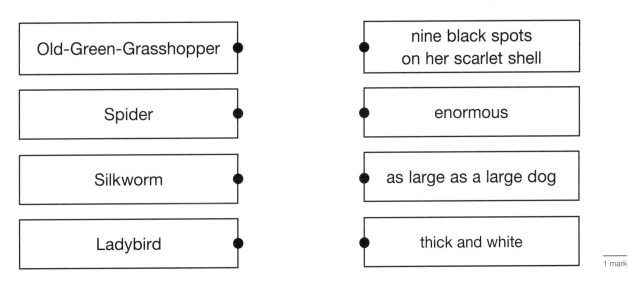

5 *He glanced behind him, thinking he could bolt back into the tunnel . . .*

What does the word *bolt* mean in this sentence?

_____

6 What reason does the Ladybird give for James looking '...*as though he's going to faint any second*'?

_____

_____

1 mark

7 Explain as fully as you can what the Ladybird means when she tells James, '*You are one of us now, didn't you know that?*'

_____

_____

1 mark

8 Put a tick in the correct box to show whether each of the following statements is **true** or **false**.

	True	False
A fence surrounded the peach.		
The tunnel was dry and cold.		
James bumped his head on the stone in the middle of the peach.		
James couldn't stand up because the peach wasn't big enough.		
The creatures were at least the same size as James.		

1 mark

9 What **effect** is the author trying to create in the sentence below?

Four pairs of round black glassy eyes were all fixed upon James.

_____

_____

_____

_____

2 marks

10 Which words does the author use to create a magical setting in the first paragraph?

Use examples from the text below.

The garden lay soft and silver in the moonlight. The grass was wet with dew and a million dewdrops were sparkling and twinkling like diamonds around his feet. And now suddenly, the whole place, the whole garden seemed to be alive with magic.

_____

_____

_____

2 marks

11 Explain why this statement by the Centipede is funny.

And meanwhile I wish you'd come over here and give me a hand with these boots. It takes me hours to get them all off by myself.

_____

_____

_____

1 mark

12 Which **two** parts of his body did James put into the peach first?

1. _____

2. _____

1 mark

13 *The floor was soggy under his knees.*

What does the word *soggy* mean in this sentence?

_____

1 mark

14 When James realised that the hole in the peach was a tunnel, how did he feel?

_____

1 mark

15 When James first entered the room at the centre of the peach, which **two** characters were seated next to the Spider?

1. _____

2. _____

1 mark

16 What type of writing is featured in this account?

Tick **one**.

diary ☐

autobiography ☐

biography ☐

story ☐

1 mark

17 Where was Floella born?

_____

1 mark

18 What does the word *challenging* mean in the sentence below?

Initially she found it very different to her life in Trinidad and growing up in two cultures was challenging.

_____

_____

1 mark

19 Floella Benjamin's family are special to her.

Find and **copy two** sentences that infer Floella had a good relationship with her parents.

Mum: _____

_____

Dad: _____

_____

2 marks

20 What is the name of Floella's autobiography?

_____

1 mark

21 What was the name of the drama in which Floella made her TV debut?

_____

1 mark

22 Find the year when each of the events below happened in Floella Benjamin's life. Write the answers in the grid below.

Event	Date
Born	
Came to England	
Made her TV debut	
Started her own television production company	
Wrote *Coming to England*	
Trekked the Great Wall of China	

2 marks

23 In what order is the text written?

Tick **one**.

importance ☐

no particular order ☐

chronological ☐

1 mark

24 For which charity does Floella raise money by running the London Marathon?

Tick **one**.

Sickle Cell Society ☐

Action for Children ☐

Barnardo's ☐

NSPCC ☐

25 This text was written to **inform** people about the life of Floella Benjamin.

Give **two** features of information writing that appear in the text.

1. _____

2. _____

26 Summarise **three** ways we know that Floella has helped children's charities.

1. _____

_____

2. _____

_____

3. _____

_____

27 Put a tick in the correct box to show whether each of the following statements about Floella is **fact** or **opinion**.

	Fact	Opinion
She worked in a bank.		
She loved her job on *Play School*.		
She presented *Play School* for 12 years.		
She has completed ten London Marathons.		
She is a keen runner.		

1 mark

28 Explain how Floella Benjamin's childhood influenced her to help young people across the world.

_____

_____

_____

2 marks

29 What happens when someone goes to investigate a crime Macavity has committed?

_____

1 mark

30 Look at the third verse.

This verse tells readers more information about Macavity's

Tick **one**.

friends.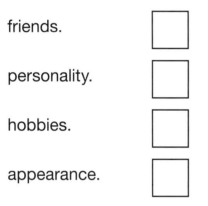

personality.

hobbies.

appearance.

1 mark

31 What does the word *neglect* mean in the third verse?

_____

_____

1 mark

32 Look at the first line of the poem.

Macavity's a Mystery Cat:

Explain why the poet describes Macavity as a *Mystery Cat*.

_____

_____

1 mark

33 Why do you think the poet uses **repetition** of the phrase *'Macavity's not there'*?

_____

_____

_____ 1 mark

34 *He always has an alibi, and one or two to spare:*

Explain what this line means.

_____

_____ 1 mark

35 What type of poem is *Macavity*?

Tick one.

limerick ☐

narrative ☐

Haiku ☐

sonnet ☐

1 mark

36 Describe the poet's use of **rhyme** throughout the poem.

_____

_____

_____

1 mark

37 *MACAVITY WASN'T THERE!*

In the final verse, why do you think the poet changed the repetition and used capital letters?

_____

_____

_____

1 mark

38 Put a tick in the correct box to show whether each of the following statements is **fact** or **opinion**.

	Fact	Opinion
It is fun watching Macavity cause trouble.		
Macavity's a ginger cat.		
His coat is dusty.		
Macavity has no-one to care for him.		

1 mark

39 **Find** and **copy** a simile from verse three.

_____

40 In verse five, **find** and **copy one** word which means the same as _stolen_.

_____

41 In the final verse, explain what the poet means by '_Just controls their operations: the Napoleon of Crime!_'

_____

_____

42 Summarise **three** main ideas the poet implies about Macavity's characteristics throughout the poem.

1. _____

_____

2. _____

_____

3. _____

_____

Key Stage 2

English grammar, punctuation and spelling

Paper 1: questions

Time:

You have **45 minutes** to complete this test paper.

Maximum mark	Actual mark
50	

First name	
Last name	

Date of birth	Day		Month		Year	

1 Circle **all** the **adjectives** in the sentence below.

The creepy shadows darted quickly past the wooden fence, along the hidden path and into the gloomy garage.

1 mark

2 Which word completes the sentence below?

You cannot go on the field today _____ it is too muddy.

Tick one.

however ☐

although ☐

because ☐

and ☐

1 mark

3 Circle one verb in each underlined pair to complete the sentence using **Standard English**.

I **did / done** a detailed piece of writing.

They **has / have** been playing outside.

1 mark

4 Rewrite the sentences below adding **apostrophes** in the correct place to mark **possession**.

The dogs tail was wagging.

_____

The boys coats were on the floor.

_____

The womens changing rooms were busy.

_____

5 Rewrite the sentence below so that it begins with the **adverbial**. Use only the same words and remember to punctuate your answer correctly.

Kenzie blew out the candles after the singing.

_____

_____

6 Add an adjective before each noun to make an **expanded noun phrase**.

The _____ skateboard park.

The _____ holiday.

7 Write the name of the punctuation circled in the sentence below.

Then, all of a sudden, lightning struck (. .) boom!

_____

1 mark

8 Insert a **semi-colon** in the most appropriate place in the sentence below.

Grace bought a bouncy ball she played with it in the garden.

1 mark

9 Tick one box in each row to show if the underlined noun is a **proper noun** or a **common noun**.

Sentence	Proper noun	Common noun
My birthday is in <u>January</u>.		
The <u>bees</u> landed on the flower.		
The car towed the <u>caravan</u>.		
His brother's name is <u>Andrew</u>.		

1 mark

10 Write a suitable **modal verb** in the sentence below.

They really _____ take more care.

1 mark

11 Change the verb below into a **noun**.

'to celebrate' _____

↑   ↑

verb   noun

1 mark

12 Draw a line to show whether each sentence is written in the **active** or **passive voice**.

| Rosie climbed the stairs. |

| passive |

| The stairs were climbed by Rosie. |

| active |

1 mark

13 Circle the **conjunction** in the sentence below.

The girls were tired but it was too early to go to bed.

1 mark

14 Circle the words in the sentence below that make it a **question**.

"You were expecting this letter today, weren't you?"

1 mark

15 Underline the **relative clause** in the sentence below.

The ice cream van that is in the car park is very popular today.

1 mark

16 Use each **preposition** from the box to complete the sentences below.

under	in	along

She walked _____ the canal path.

The dog hid _____ the table.

I was lost _____ the maze.

1 mark

17 Which sentence contains **two verbs**?

Tick **one**.

I ran home very quickly. ☐

The teacher read a very long story. ☐

The little boy watched TV and ate a sandwich. ☐

The spider crawled underneath the doormat. ☐

1 mark

18 Circle **all** the **determiners** in the sentence below.

An alligator is a large reptile.

1 mark

19 Complete the sentence using suitable **pronouns**.

Rosie's homework was too hard for _____ and

_____ felt sad that _____

couldn't do it.

1 mark

20 Which of the events in the sentences below is the **most** likely to happen?

Tick **one**.

We might go to the cinema tonight. ☐

He will go to school tomorrow. ☐

They could go camping at the weekend. ☐

I can go to your party tomorrow. ☐

1 mark

21 Write a suitable **question tag** at the end of the statements below.

It's a nice day today, _____

You like reading, _____

1 mark

22 Insert a set of **brackets** so that the sentence below is punctuated correctly.

Mrs Jones the Year 5 teacher played the piano in school today.

1 mark

23 Add a **subordinate clause** to the main clause below.

_____, I went

to the park.

1 mark

24 Insert a **comma** in the correct place in the sentence below.

Hanging upside down the bat made loud noises as the night sky grew darker.

1 mark

25 Complete the table by inserting a **synonym** and an **antonym**.

Word	Synonym	Antonym
stiff		
angry		

1 mark

26 Circle the correct form of the underlined **verb** in each sentence.

The tree **sway / sways** gently in the breeze.

The goats **have / has** two horns each.

The children **are / is** too noisy!

1 mark

27 To make a pop-up book, Louis needs three pieces of equipment: scissors, card and glue.
Rewrite this sentence as an instruction using a **colon** and **bullet points**.

To make a pop-up book you will need three things

_____

_____

_____

1 mark

28 Choose a suitable **prefix** for the following verbs:

_____ cover

_____ place

_____ allow

1 mark

29 Write **two conjunctions** to complete the sentence below.

I like drawing _____ painting

_____ my sister prefers writing.

1 mark

30 Rewrite the sentence below so that it begins with an **adverbial**.
Remember to punctuate your sentence correctly.

We went to the cinema after tea.

_____

1 mark

31 Rewrite the sentence below using **direct speech**.
Remember to punctuate your sentence correctly.

Mrs Shepherd told her class there will be an important visitor in assembly.

_____

_____

1 mark

32 Put **commas** in the correct places to separate items in the list below.

The milkman delivers fresh produce on a Monday Tuesday Thursday
and Saturday.

1 mark

33 Add the pronouns **I** and **me** to the sentences below to make them
correct.

Noah and _____ went for a walk in the woods.

Our parents told my sister and _____ to hurry up.

1 mark

34 Circle the **preposition** in the sentence.

The cat slept in the warm, cosy basket.

1 mark

35 Which of the sentences below uses the **semi-colon** correctly?

Tick **one**.

Ella played the piano; Alex played the flute. ☐

Ella played; the piano Alex played; the flute. ☐

Ella played; the piano; Alex played the flute. ☐

Ella; played the piano Alex; played the flute. ☐

1 mark

36 Put a tick in each row to show if the words on the left are **adverbs of time** or **place**.

Adverb	Time (when)	Place (where)
frequently		
regularly		
often		
in the middle of		

1 mark

37 Underline the **relative clause** in the sentence below.

Brighton, which is a seaside town, is located on the south coast of England.

1 mark

38 Add the words from the boxes below to this sentence starter to make **one** sentence.
Remember to punctuate your answer correctly.

when she got a puppy for her birthday	was thrilled
who loves dogs	Hayley

My best friend _____

_____

1 mark

39 Write this sentence as **direct speech** using **inverted commas**.

I told my brother it was my turn next.

_____

1 mark

40 Contract these words using an **apostrophe**.

should have _____

they will _____

he is _____

1 mark

41 Insert the correct punctuation into this sentence.
The first one has been done for you.

D
~~d~~uring his stay on the farm jon saw some ducks a herd of goats and a huge pink pig

1 mark

42 Put a tick in each row to show whether each **explanation** is **true** or **false**.

Explanation	True	False
A <u>request</u> is to ask for something.		
An <u>indulgent</u> is an invitation.		
A <u>container</u> is used to put things in.		
A <u>bleak</u> morning is a dismal one.		

1 mark

43 Write the **basic form** of each verb.

laughs, laughed = to _____

walks, walked = to _____

flies, flew = to _____

grows, grew = to _____

1 mark

44 Rewrite the sentence below using **Standard English**.

I've not got none.

_____

45 Complete the table below by adding a **suffix** to each verb to make a **noun**.

Verb	Noun
agree	
refer	
form	
assist	

46 What does the root word <u>fin</u> mean in the word family below?

finite	infinity	finish

Tick one.

beginning ☐

distant ☐

end ☐

nearby ☐

47 Underline the **modal verb** in the sentence below.

We should have stayed late at school tonight.

48 Rewrite the sentence below, changing it to the **past progressive tense**.

I eat all my dinner.

_____

1 mark

49 The sentence below has an **apostrophe** missing.
Rewrite the sentence and **explain** why the apostrophe is needed.

Annies mum worked at the school library.

_____

_____

_____

1 mark

50 Which word completes the sentence so that it uses the **subjunctive mood**?

The Head Teacher said, "If there _____ to be a fire, students should exit through the rear doors."

Tick **one**.

was ☐

were ☐

had ☐

going ☐

1 mark

SET
B

English
grammar,
punctuation
and spelling

PAPER 2

Key Stage 2

English grammar, punctuation and spelling

Paper 2: spelling

You will need to ask someone to read the instructions and sentences to you. These can be found on pages 101–102.

Time:

You have approximately **15 minutes** to complete this test paper.

Maximum mark	Actual mark
20	

First name	
Last name	

Date of birth	Day		Month		Year	

Spelling

1 The _____ of Majorca is close to Spain.

2 The chocolate cake was _____.

3 _____ can be mashed, chipped, boiled or baked.

4 A _____ should never be broken!

5 My _____ sport is cricket.

6 The _____ of the luggage is less than 15 kilograms.

7 _____ teachers have told me I have a talent for drawing.

8 The kittens are _____.

9 Playing football for the school team is a great _____.

10 All the _____ information should be underlined.

11 I am trying to _____ my mum to buy me some new boots.

12 My _____ feels full after lunch.

13 Mata listened to the story with _____.

14 The first time we met was a little _____.

15 Ned's _____ was the fastest.

16 The whole family is in _____ for our pet.

17 Because of the roadworks, the traffic was _____.

18 Coffee and fizzy drinks usually contain _____.

19 The gymnasts _____ their weight across the bars.

20 We do not mind what type of _____ we stay in on holiday.

Contents

English reading booklets

Set A

A Mad Tea Party 76

The Isles of Scilly 78

Street Child 81

Set B

James and the Giant Peach 86

About Floella 89

Macavity 91

Answers and mark scheme 93

Spelling test administration 101

Reading booklet

Contents

A Mad Tea Party

pages 76–77

The Isles of Scilly

pages 78–80

Street Child

pages 81–83

A Mad Tea Party

Alice has just drunk a magic potion, which has made her very small. It enables her to enter Wonderland, where nothing is ever quite as it seems!

The scene begins in the garden. There is a table under a tree in front of a house. The March Hare and the Hatter are having tea at the table. A dormouse sits between them.

Narrator: The March Hare and the Mad Hatter are having tea, all squashed at one end of a very large table.

Alice: Hello, mind if I join you all?

Hare, Hatter, Dormouse: No room! No room!

Alice: What are you talking about, there's plenty of room.

Alice sits down.

Hare: Have some wine.

Alice: *(looking around the table)* I don't see any wine.

Hare: There isn't any.

Alice: *(in an angry voice)* Then it wasn't very civil of you to offer it!

Hare: It wasn't very civil of you to sit down without being invited.

Alice: I didn't know it was your table, it's laid for many more than three.

Hatter: *(looking up and down at Alice)* Your hair wants cutting.

Alice: You should learn not to make personal remarks. It's very rude!

Narrator: The characters continue arguing until the Hatter opens his eyes very wide and begins talking in riddles.

Hatter: Why is a raven like a writing desk?

Alice: I believe I can guess that.

Hare: Do you mean you think you can find the answer for it?

Alice: Exactly so.

Hare: Then you should say what you mean.

Alice: I do. At least, I mean what I say – that's the same thing you know.

Hatter: Not the same thing a bit! Why, you might just as well say that I like what I get is the same as I get what I like.

Dormouse: *(talking in a sleepy way)* I breathe when I sleep is the same thing as I sleep when I breathe!

Hatter: It is the same thing with you!

Narrator: The conversation drops, and the party sits silently for a minute.

(The Hatter takes his watch out of his pocket and looks at it uneasily; he shakes it and holds it to his ear. He then dips it in his cup of tea and looks at it again.)

The Isles of Scilly

The Isles of Scilly

Location

The Isles of Scilly are a group of islands located 45 km (28 miles) off the coast of the Cornish peninsula.

The Islands

The Isles of Scilly are made up of five inhabited and approximately 140 other islands. The largest of the islands is called St Mary's, with Tresco, St Martin's, St Agnes and Bryher being the others.

The main settlement on St Mary's is Hugh Town. This is a very small town with only a few shops, banks, restaurants, hotels and pubs. The population of Hugh Town is just over 1000.

Travel

Because the Isles of Scilly are so small, very few people own cars. Locals usually walk or ride bicycles. Public transport is a boat service between the islands.

To reach the Isles of Scilly from the mainland, visitors need to travel on either a small aeroplane (Skybus) or a passenger ferry (*The Scillonian*). These methods of transport are both an amazing experience for travellers to the islands and the table below lists the advantages and disadvantages of each.

	Skybus	**The Scillonian**
Advantages	Travel to and from three different mainland airports	Cafés serving hot and cold food on board
	Bird's-eye views of the islands	Often see dolphins, sea birds and basking sharks
	Quick	Seaside views
	Small and personal	Cheap
Disadvantages	Limited luggage allowed	Often rough seas and passengers may suffer motion sickness
	More expensive	Longer journey
	Flights can be cancelled because of high winds	

Weather

The Isles of Scilly have a unique climate, with the mildest and warmest temperatures in the United Kingdom. The average annual temperature is 11.8 °C (53.2 °F) in comparison to London, where it is 11.6 °C (52.9 °F).

The winters in Scilly are relatively warm and the islands very rarely get frosts or snow. They are however windy, due to the full force of the wind off the Atlantic Ocean.

Plants and Animals

The warm, humid climate of the Isles of Scilly allows a variety of rare plants and flowers to grow, which are not seen in other parts of the United Kingdom.

Some people describe the Scilly Islands as 'a large natural greenhouse'. Even in winter, there are hundreds of different plants in bloom.

Month	Jan	Feb	Mar	Apr	May	Jun	Jul	Aug	Sept	Oct	Nov	Dec
Average temp. °C (°F)	8.0 (46.4)	7.9 (46.2)	8.8 (47.8)	9.8 (49.6)	12.0 (53.5)	14.5 (58.1)	16.5 (61.7)	16.9 (62.5)	15.5 (59.8)	12.7 (54.8)	10.3 (50.6)	8.7 (47.6)

Because of the warm temperatures, many birds migrate to Scilly. Some birds stop off on their way across the Atlantic Ocean, while others stay on the islands. There are many different types of birds on the islands, ranging from common birds such as sparrows, thrushes and gulls, to more unusual birds like puffins, cuckoos and wheatears.

Tourism

The Isles of Scilly rely on tourism. The majority of shops, restaurants, bars and cafés earn money from visitors during the summer season. People travel to Scilly for many reasons. Quite often there are visitors who come on walking holidays, bird-watching trips and to relax on one of the quiet beaches.

Holidaymakers can choose accommodation suitable for their stay. The main islands have a choice of hotels, bed and breakfasts, self-catering cottages and camping facilities.

Activities

Many people choose to participate in water sports, including sailing, kayaking, boating and fishing.

The islands are famous for their clear waters, which also make snorkelling and diving popular activities.

'Gig racing' is the main sport on the Isles of Scilly. Gigs are traditional working boats, which six or seven people sit inside and row. Many islanders take part in gig practices and races throughout the season.

People watch the races and cheer on the gigs from passenger boats that follow the race or they sometimes watch the finish from the quay on St Mary's. The Isles of Scilly host an annual gig championship; thousands of rowers from as far away as Holland flock to the island to race at this event.

Historic Sites

The Isles of Scilly have many historic landmarks waiting to be explored, including castles, churches, lighthouses and ruins. There are art galleries and exhibitions, museums and often concerts to attend.

Probably the most impressive feature of the Isles of Scilly is its natural beauty; the swirling golden beaches, sand dunes, rocky coastlines and scenic views are well worth a visit.

Reading booklet

SET
B

English
reading

READING
BOOKLET

Contents

James and the Giant Peach

pages 86–88

About Floella

pages 89–90

Macavity

pages 91–92

James and the Giant Peach

The garden lay soft and silver in the moonlight. The grass was wet with dew and a million dewdrops were sparkling and twinkling like diamonds around his feet. And now suddenly, the whole place, the whole garden seemed to be *alive* with magic.

Almost without knowing what he was doing, as though drawn by some powerful magnet, James Henry Trotter started walking slowly towards the giant peach. He climbed over the fence that surrounded it, and stood directly beneath it, staring up at its great bulging sides. He put out a hand and touched it gently with the tip of one finger. It felt soft and warm and slightly furry, like the skin of a baby mouse. He moved a step closer and rubbed his cheek lightly against the soft skin. And then suddenly, while he was doing this, he happened to notice that right beside him and below him, close to the ground, there was a hole in the side of the peach.

It was quite a large hole, the sort of thing an animal about the size of a fox might have made.

James knelt down in front of it and poked his head and shoulders inside.

He crawled in.

He kept on crawling.

This isn't just a hole, he thought excitedly. It's a tunnel!

The tunnel was damp and murky, and all around him there was the curious bittersweet smell of fresh peach. The floor was soggy under his knees, the walls were wet and sticky, and peach juice was dripping from the ceiling. James opened his mouth and caught some of it on his tongue. It tasted delicious.

He was crawling uphill now, as though the tunnel were leading straight towards the very centre of the gigantic fruit. Every few seconds he paused and took a bite out of the wall. The peach flesh was sweet and juicy, and marvellously refreshing.

He crawled on for several more yards, and then suddenly – bang – the top of his head bumped into something extremely hard blocking his way. He glanced up. In front of him there was a solid wall that seemed at first as though it were made of wood. He touched it with his fingers. It certainly felt like wood, except that it was very jagged and full of deep grooves.

'Good heavens!' he said. 'I know what this is! I've come to the stone in the middle of the peach!'

Then he noticed that there was a small door cut into the face of the peach stone. He gave a push. It swung open. He crawled through it, and before he had time to glance up and see where he was, he heard a voice saying, 'Look who's here!' And another one said, 'We've been waiting for you!'

James stopped and stared at the speakers, his face white with horror.

He started to stand up, but his knees were shaking so much he had to sit down again on the floor. He glanced behind him, thinking he could bolt back into the tunnel the way he had come, but the doorway had disappeared. There was now only a solid brown wall behind him.

James's large frightened eyes travelled slowly around the room.

The creatures, some sitting on chairs, others reclining on a sofa, were all watching him intently.

Creatures?

Or were they insects?

An insect is usually something rather small, is it not? A grasshopper, for example, is an insect.

So what would you call it if you saw a grasshopper as large as a dog? As large as a *large* dog. You could hardly call *that* an insect, could you?

There was an Old-Green-Grasshopper as large as a large dog sitting on a stool directly across the room from James now.

And next to the Old-Green-Grasshopper, there was an enormous Spider.

And next to the Spider, there was a giant Ladybird with nine black spots on her scarlet shell.

Each of these three was squatting upon a magnificent chair.

On a sofa near by, reclining comfortably in curled-up positions, there was a Centipede and an Earthworm.

On the floor over in the far corner, there was something thick and white that looked as though it might be a Silkworm. But it was sleeping soundly and nobody was paying any attention to it.

Every one of these 'creatures' was at least as big as James himself, and in the strange greenish light that shone down from somewhere in the ceiling, they were absolutely terrifying to behold.

'I'm hungry!' the Spider announced suddenly, staring hard at James.

'*I'm* famished!' the Old-Green-Grasshopper said.

'So am *I*!' the Ladybird cried.

The Centipede sat up a little straighter on the sofa. '*Everyone's* famished!' he said. 'We need food!'

Four pairs of round black glassy eyes were all fixed upon James.

The Centipede made a wriggling movement with his body as though he were about to glide off the sofa – but he didn't.

There was a long pause – and a long silence.

The Spider (who happened to be a female spider) opened her mouth and ran a long black tongue delicately over her lips. 'Aren't you hungry?' she asked suddenly, leaning forward and addressing herself to James.

Poor James was backed up against the far wall, shivering with fright and much too terrified to answer.

'What's the matter with you?' the Old-Green-Grasshopper asked. 'You look positively ill!'

'He looks as though he's going to faint any second,' the Centipede said.

'Oh, my goodness, the poor thing!' the Ladybird cried. 'I do believe he thinks it's *him* that we are wanting to eat!' There was a roar of laughter from all sides.

'Oh dear, oh dear!' they said. 'What an awful thought!'

'You mustn't be frightened,' the Ladybird said kindly. 'We wouldn't dream of hurting you. You are one of us now, didn't you know that? You are one of the crew. We're all in the same boat.'

'We've been waiting for you all day long,' the Old-Green-Grasshopper said. 'We thought you were never going to turn up. I'm glad you made it.'

'So cheer up, my boy, cheer up!' the Centipede said. 'And meanwhile I wish you'd come over here and give me a hand with these boots. It takes me *hours* to get them all off by myself.'

About Floella

Floella Benjamin was born in the Caribbean on an island called Trinidad on 23rd September 1949. Her father decided to emigrate to England and she came to join him in 1960, when she was 11 years old. Floella's family started their life in Great Britain in Beckenham, South London. Initially she found it very different to her life in Trinidad and growing up in two cultures was challenging.

Floella's mother (Marmie) was a great inspiration to her. She gave her lots of love and encouraged her to do well at school.

Floella always dreamed of becoming a teacher, but instead ended up working in a bank and then later starred in stage musicals. While Floella enjoyed being on stage, she also wanted to try working in television so she auditioned for a variety of roles. Her TV debut was in 1974 in a drama called *Within these Walls* and her success in the show landed her many more roles in TV dramas.

Floella then took on a new role as a presenter of *Play School*, a 1970s children's show. She loved this job and presented the programme for 12 years.

As well as acting and presenting, Floella also loves to sing. She began singing with her dad who had a jazz band.

She often sang with her dad's band and also with large classical orchestras.

In 1987 Floella started her own television production company.

Next page ▶▶▶

Floella has also starred in several pantomimes, worked on numerous radio programmes, narrated audio books and has done voiceovers for a range of adverts and commercials.

Since 1983, Floella has written over 25 children's books.

One book Floella is particularly proud of is one that has been made into a film. *Coming to England* was written in 1995 and is based on her own life. In the book Floella talks about what it's like to be different, to move countries and change cultures and her feelings of rejection. The drama *Coming to England* won a Royal Television Society Award in 2004.

Floella is a keen runner who has completed ten London Marathons for the children's charity Barnardo's. This achievement is even more special as until she turned 50 years old, Floella had never even run at all!

Trekking the Great Wall of China in 2004 in aid of NCH Action for Children is another one of Floella's achievements. She started this in the Gobi Desert and finished 400 km later where the Great Wall meets the Yellow Sea.

Today Floella's passion is for inspiring and helping children and young people. She is a patron and supporter of many charities, including Action for Children and the Sickle Cell Society. In 2008, Floella was inducted into the National Society for the Prevention of Cruelty to Children (NSPCC) Hall of Fame.

Floella supports and empathises with children and young people across the world. Through her charity work, her writing and personal attitudes, she strives to help young people find their identity and to understand where they come from. She hopes all children have a sense of belonging and learn to become proud of themselves.

Macavity

Macavity's a Mystery Cat: he's called the Hidden Paw –
    For he's the master criminal who can defy the Law.
He's the bafflement of Scotland Yard, the Flying Squad's despair:
    For when they reach the scene of crime – *Macavity's not there!*

Macavity, Macavity, there's no one like Macavity,
    He's broken every human law, he breaks the law of gravity.
His powers of levitation would make a fakir stare,
    And when you reach the scene of crime – Macavity's not there!
You may seek him in the basement, you may look up in the air –
    But I tell you once and once again, *Macavity's not there!*

Macavity's a ginger cat, he's very tall and thin;
    You would know him if you saw him, for his eyes are sunken in.
His brow is deeply lined with thought, his head is highly domed;
    His coat is dusty from neglect, his whiskers are uncombed.
He sways his head from side to side, with movements like a snake;
    And when you think he's half asleep, he's always wide awake.

Macavity, Macavity, there's no one like Macavity,
    For he's a fiend in feline shape, a monster of depravity.
You may meet him in a by-street, you may see him in the square –
    But when a crime's discovered, then *Macavity's not there!*

He's outwardly respectable. (They say he cheats at cards.)
    And his footprints are not found in any file of Scotland Yard's.
And when the larder's looted, or the jewel-case is rifled,
    Or when the milk is missing, or another Peke's been stifled,
Or the greenhouse glass is broken, and the trellis past repair –
    Ay, there's the wonder of the thing! *Macavity's not there!*

And when the Foreign Office find a Treaty's gone astray,
  Or the Admiralty lose some plans and drawings by the way,
There may be a scrap of paper in the hall or on the stair –
  But it's useless to investigate – *Macavity's not there!*
And when the loss has been disclosed, the Secret Service say:
  'It *must* have been Macavity!' – but he's a mile away.
You'll be sure to find him resting, or a-licking of his thumbs,
  Or engaged in doing complicated long division sums.

Macavity, Macavity, there's no one like Macavity,
  There never was a Cat of such deceitfulness and suavity.
He always has an alibi, and one or two to spare:
  At whatever time the deed took place – MACAVITY WASN'T THERE!
And they say that all the Cats whose wicked deeds are widely known,
  (I might mention Mungojerrie, I might mention Griddlebone)
Are nothing more than agents for the Cat who all the time
  Just controls their operations: the Napoleon of Crime!

Answers

Set A English reading

A Mad Tea Party

1. Accept either in the garden or in Wonderland. **(1 mark)**
2. She has just drunk a magic potion that makes her small. **(1 mark)**
3. …there's plenty of room. **(1 mark)**
4. the Hare **(1 mark)**
5. polite **(1 mark)**
6. ' …all squashed at one end of a very large table.' **(1 mark)**
7. Any one of the following points:
   - Alice thinks personal remarks are rude.
   - The Hatter's remarks are said very abruptly and to the point.
   - The Hatter's remarks are unprovoked.
   (1 mark)
8. The Mad Hatter begins talking in riddles. **(1 mark)**
9. Any one from: lowers; they become quiet; ends. **(1 mark)**
10. Any one from: confident; friendly; determined; argumentative; sensible. **(1 mark)**
11. Any one from: a narrator; new line for each speaker; stage directions; use of direct language; set as a scene; no speech marks. **(1 mark)**
12. Any one from: it is a tea party which is very unusual; the characters are acting in strange ways; they are saying mad things; they are sitting squashed up; they are talking in riddles; they are offering wine which isn't there. **(1 mark)**
13. Any one from: Alice sits down; looking around the table; in an angry voice; looking up and down at Alice; talking in a sleepy way. **(1 mark)**
14. puzzle **(1 mark)**
15. Any one from: the Narrator sets the scene; moves the story forward; explains what's happening; introduces characters. **(1 mark)**
16. *An Unusual Tea Party* **(1 mark)**

The Isles of Scilly

17. St Mary's **(1 mark)**
18. people live there **(1 mark)**
19. a small aeroplane (Skybus); a passenger ferry (*The Scillonian*)
    (1 mark: both correct for 1 mark)
20. A day visitor with no luggage would be best taking the aeroplane (Skybus) because it's quicker and they would have longer to spend in the Isles of Scilly. They have no luggage so can travel by aeroplane. They will get a good view of all the islands even though they will not get time to see them all on foot. They will be able to choose one of three airports to travel from on the mainland.
    (1 mark for any point from above)

    A family staying for a week who want to see dolphins swimming would be best taking the passenger ferry because they may be able to see dolphins (and basking sharks and sea birds) from the ferry. They are staying a whole week so have plenty of time to spend travelling to Scilly by boat. The family might want to buy food or drinks on board and, as the boat is cheaper, it will cost them less.
    (1 mark for any point from above)
21. There are lots of them, they are not unusual or rare. **(1 mark)**
22. Any of the following answers are acceptable but they must be consistently either 'yes' or 'no'.
    Yes:
    - They are small.
    - Not many cars – good to get away from lots of traffic.
    - Enjoy boats, walking or cycling.
    - Lots of wildlife – birds, fish and plants to see.
    - Lots of tourism.
    - Relaxing; peaceful; quiet.
    - Lovely beaches, sand dunes, rocky coastlines.
    - Varied accommodation.
    - Water sports available.
    - Want to watch the gig races.
    - Would like to explore castles, churches, lighthouses.
    - Would like to visit art galleries, exhibitions, museums, attend concerts.
    - Beautiful islands.
    - Amazing views.
    - Warm climate.

    No:
    - Difficult to get to – you can't drive.

- Very quiet – not many people live there.
- The main town does not have many large facilities.
- Not keen on water, boats or water sports.
- Would prefer somewhere not as warm.
- No interest in birds or wildlife.
- Not much to do.

  (1 mark: all three correct for 1 mark)

23. Participating: a participant would sit inside the gig; row; take part in races.
    Watching: a spectator would watch the race from a boat, or from the quay on St Mary's; cheer on the gigs.

    (2 marks: 1 mark for one participating point, 1 mark for one watching point)

24. Any two of the following:
- maps
- charts
- headings / subheadings
- present tense
- facts are used
- clear language.   **(2 marks)**

25. Any three from: walking; bird watching; relaxing on beaches; water sports; visiting historic sites; enjoying the wildlife / plants.

    (1 mark for three correct answers)

26. Any two from: walk; ride bicycles; by boat.

    (1 mark)

27. a travel leaflet   **(1 mark)**

28.

Language used	Explanation of the effect of the language
. . . *flock to the island to race.*	It makes the reader think rowers group like a flock of sheep or birds, and that there are lots of them.
. . . *waiting to be explored* . . .	This phrase gives readers an image of the buildings waiting for people to visit them – really the buildings are just standing there – the author adds interest.
. . . *swirling golden beaches* . . .	Conjures up a picture of the wind gently blowing the sand, which swirls into dunes. 'Golden' makes the reader think of a sunny, warm day, making the beach inviting.

(3 marks)

Street Child

29. A workhouse   **(1 mark)**
30. He doesn't know life anywhere else.   **(1 mark)**
31. Any one from: so that the children can't escape; so that the children can't see out; so no one can see in.   **(1 mark)**
32. Any one from: He could tell the time of year by the weather; the colour of the sky; the light, and dark mornings and nights; he is aware of the change in the seasons.   **(1 mark)**
33. He can't stay here forever or for another year; he needs to escape so he will try to run away.

    (1 mark for either point)

34. pulled   **(1 mark)**
35. Any one from: he knew he had plans to run away; he wasn't going to be there much longer, he had more important things to think about; this would be his last beating so he felt positive and thought he could deal with anything.   **(1 mark)**
36. He was afraid they'll get caught and get thrashed.   **(1 mark)**
37. **Yes:** Jim is daft for thinking he can escape the workhouse; for running away; for thinking he can go with the big boys – he'll get caught and then get another terrible beating; he has no real plans – where will he sleep? How will he eat?
    No: Jim isn't daft for having dreams or for trying to find a way out of the workhouse.   **(1 mark)**
38. Look out for each other: 'Don't go, Jim.' Care for each other: 'Tip passed his own share along to him.' Trust each other: Jim told Tip his plans – 'Tip, I'm going to run away today. Come with me?' Strong friendship: they suffer the workhouse together.

    (2 marks: award 1 mark for each correct point)

39. He doesn't remember / know life anywhere else.   **(1 mark)**

40.

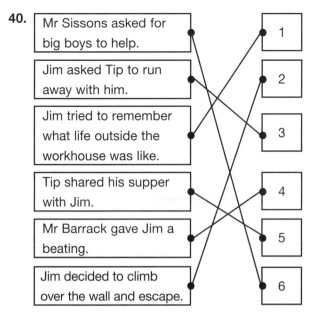

Mr Sissons asked for big boys to help.	1
Jim asked Tip to run away with him.	2
Jim tried to remember what life outside the workhouse was like.	3
Tip shared his supper with Jim.	4
Mr Barrack gave Jim a beating.	5
Jim decided to climb over the wall and escape.	6

(1 mark for all correct)

41. joy, triumphant

(1 mark: both correct for 1 mark)

42.

Language used	Explanation of the effect of the language
Jim's wild thoughts *drummed inside* *him . . .*	The thoughts were pounding away – beating / niggling / constantly there inside him – they were like a drum beat – loud / strong / constant.
. . . the beating *inside him was like* *a wild bird now . . .*	His thoughts were getting stronger – like a wild bird's wings – they were spreading out – he was thinking more about it – he couldn't contain his thoughts any more – they needed to escape and fly like a bird – be released.
. . . a shimmer of *pain and thrumming* *wings.*	A sudden burst of pain – his 'wings' had been damaged due to the beating he had just endured – he was hurt.

(3 marks: 1 mark for each correct box)

Set A English grammar, punctuation and spelling

Paper 1: questions

1. an elephant; a superhero

   (1 mark: both correct for 1 mark)

2. discover **(1 mark)**

3. We **was /** ⃝**were** going to play outside on our bikes. I **done /** ⃝**did** well in my maths test this morning. **(1 mark)**

4. "Wait for me!" shouted Orla. "Ouch! My hand hurts." Freddie whispered, "Are you scared?" **(1 mark)**

5. Olivia and Sandip ⃝**were building** sandcastles at the beach. **(1 mark)**

6. The authors wrote letters to the newspaper. **(1 mark)**

7. Nottingham is located in the East Midlands. The river that runs through Nottingham is called the River Trent. **(1 mark)**

8. ⃝**Since** it was very cold outside, Sam decided to fasten his coat. **(1 mark)**

9.

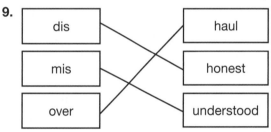

dis	haul
mis	honest
over	understood

(1 mark)

10. Emma's cat had five kittens last night. The boys' changing rooms were locked. Jamie's lunchbox was left overnight in his classroom. **(1 mark)**

11. William Shakespeare – a famous author – wrote the play 'Macbeth'. **(1 mark)**

12. Although she is younger than me, my sister is much taller. **(1 mark)**

13. Any suitable adverbials of time, e.g. First; Then; Next, followed by a comma. **(1 mark)**

14. You've been learning about materials in science, haven't you? **(1 mark)**

15. While the band was playing, I was dancing with my friends. **(1 mark)**

16. therefore **(1 mark)**

17. Feeling confident, the pianist played to a room full of people. **(1 mark)**

18. whipped **(1 mark)**

19. pronoun **(1 mark)**

20. I will wash the car today. **(1 mark)**

21.

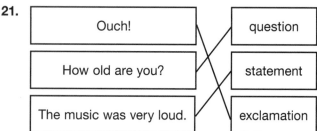

Ouch!	question
How old are you?	statement
The music was very loud.	exclamation

(1 mark: all correct for 1 mark)

22. (he) **(1 mark)**

23. Later that evening, we said goodbye and began our journey home. **(1 mark)**

24. Mangoes, kiwis, apples, pineapples and strawberries are all types of fruit.
(1 mark: all correct for 1 mark)

25. We laughed at each other's funny jokes. **(1 mark)**

26. I am allowed to watch television (while) eating my dinner. **(1 mark)**

27. Answers may vary. Examples:

	Synonym	Antonym
sad	unhappy	happy
rich	wealthy	poor
big	large	small
old	ancient	new

(1 mark)

28. The skateboard park, located behind the playground, is to be used by children who are over eight. **Or** The skateboard park (located behind the playground) is to be used by children who are over eight. **Or** The skateboard park – located behind the playground – is to be used by children who are over eight. **(1 mark)**

29. On your marks . . . ready . . . steady . . . go! **(1 mark)**

30. The historians visited the ancient ruins. **(1 mark)**

31.

Noun	Verb
simplification	to simplify
calculation	to calculate
magnification	to magnify

(1 mark)

32. The girl walked (up) the stairs. **(1 mark)**

33. Any correct addition of a subordinate clause will be award a mark, e.g. Despite the cold, rainy morning, the farmer went into his field; The farmer, who owned several acres of land, went into his field. **(1 mark)**

34. My uncle, who lives in France, came to visit us at Christmas. **Or** My uncle who lives in France came to visit us at Christmas. **Or** At Christmas, my uncle who lives in France came to visit us. **Or** At Christmas, my uncle, who lives in France, came to visit us. **(1 mark)**

35. The old lady <u>who was shouting at her neighbour</u> was feeling angry. **(1 mark)**

36. Any suitable question starting with a capital letter and ending with a question mark, e.g. How does Joel get to school? **(1 mark)**

37. (Put) (Mix) **(1 mark: both correct for 1 mark)**

38. He **(1 mark)**

39. Any one from: can't; won't; didn't; don't; couldn't; wouldn't. **(1 mark)**

40.

to dance	to smile

When I was dancing in the show I was smiling all the time.

(2 marks: 1 mark for each correct word)

41. "What time does the train leave the station?" Mary asked the guard.
"Three minutes past ten" the guard answered.
(1 mark for both sentences correct)

42. 'Where are you going' the bus driver asked.

(1 mark)

43. The books **and** DVDs need returning to the library on Monday **or** Tuesday **but** remember it is closed each day for lunch. **(1 mark for all correct)**

44. While I was waiting to see the doctor, I read a book. **(1 mark)**

45. The cat – fast asleep on the rug – was keeping warm by the fire. **(1 mark)**

46. <u>With his sports kit on,</u> Tom was ready for the game. **(1 mark)**

47. If the bus were late again, the children would be cross. **(1 mark)**

48.

Noun	Adjective
child	childish/childlike
courage	courageous
despair	desperate
hope	hopeful
caution	cautious

(1 mark)

49. around **(1 mark)**

50. went; were **(1 mark)**

Set B English grammar, punctuation and spelling

Paper 1: questions

1. The (creepy) shadows darted quickly past the (wooden) fence, along the (hidden) path and into the (gloomy) garage. **(1 mark for all correct)**
2. because **(1 mark)**
3. (did); (have) **(1 mark for both correct)**
4. The dog's tail was wagging.
   The boys' coats were on the floor.
   The women's changing rooms were busy.
   (1 mark for all correct)
5. After the singing, Kenzie blew out the candles.
   (1 mark)
6. Any correct answer, e.g.
   The busy skateboard park.
   The skiing holiday. **(1 mark for all correct)**
7. ellipses **(1 mark)**
8. Grace bought a bouncy ball; she played with it in the garden. **(1 mark)**
9.

Sentence	Proper noun	Common noun
My birthday is in January.	✓	
The bees landed on the flower.		✓
The car towed the caravan.		✓
His brother's name is Andrew.	✓	

   (1 mark for all correct)
10. Any suitable modal verb, e.g. should;
    ought (to) **(1 mark)**
11. noun = 'celebration' **(1 mark)**
12.

   Rosie climbed the stairs. — passive
   The stairs were climbed by Rosie. — active
   (1 mark for both correct)
13. The girls were tired (but) it was too early to go to bed. **(1 mark)**
14. "You were expecting this letter today, (weren't you?)" **(1 mark)**
15. The ice cream van that is in the car park is very popular today. **(1 mark)**

16. She walked along the canal path.
    The dog hid under the table.
    I was lost in the maze. **(1 mark for all correct)**
17. The little boy watched TV and ate a sandwich.
    (1 mark)
18. (An) alligator is (a) large reptile.
    (1 mark for both correct)
19. Rosie's homework was too hard for **her** and **she** felt sad that **she** couldn't do **it**.
    (1 mark for all correct)
20. He will go to school tomorrow. **(1 mark)**
21. Isn't it?; don't you?
    (1 mark for both correct)
22. Mrs Jones (the Year 5 teacher) played the piano in school today. **(1 mark)**
23. Any suitable subordinate clauses, e.g. Although I didn't have much time, I went to the park.
    (1 mark)
24. Hanging upside down, the bat made loud noises as the night sky grew darker. **(1 mark)**
25. Any suitable words, e.g.

Word	Synonym	Antonym
stiff	rigid	bendy
angry	cross	calm

   (1 mark for all words if correct)
26. The tree **sway** / (sways) gently in the breeze.
    The goats (have) / **has** two horns each.
    The children (are) / **is** too noisy!
    (1 mark for all correct)
27. To make a pop-up book you will need three things:
    • scissors
    • card
    • glue
    (Accept full-stop after each word. Accept capital letter at start of each word)
    (1 mark: 1 mark if all bullet points are correct)
28. Any three from:
    dis / re / un   cover
    re   place
    dis   allow **(1 mark for all correct)**
29. I like drawing **and** painting **but / although** my sister prefers writing.
    (1 mark for both correct)
30. After tea, we went to the cinema.
    (1 mark for correct adverbial and correct punctuation)

31. "There will be an important visitor in assembly," Mrs Shepherd told her class. **Or** Mrs Shepherd told her class, "There will be an important visitor in assembly." **(1 mark)**

32. The milkman delivers fresh produce on a Monday, Tuesday, Thursday and Saturday. **(1 mark)**

33. Noah and **I** went for a walk in the woods. Our parents told my sister and **me** to hurry up. **(1 mark)**

34. The cat slept (in) the warm, cosy basket. **(1 mark)**

35. Ella played the piano; Alex played the flute. **(1 mark)**

36.

Adverbial	Time (when)	Place (where)
frequently	✓	
regularly	✓	
often	✓	
in the middle of		✓

(1 mark for all correct)

37. Brighton, which is a seaside town, is located on the south coast of England. **(1 mark)**

38. My best friend, Hayley, who loves dogs, was thrilled when she got a puppy for her birthday. **Or** My best friend Hayley, who loves dogs, was thrilled when she got a puppy for her birthday. **(1 mark)**

39. 'It's my turn next,' I told my older brother. **(1 mark)**

40. should've; they'll; he's **(1 mark for all correct)**

41. During his stay on the farm, Jon saw some ducks, a herd of goats and a huge, pink pig. Accept a colon after 'saw'. **(1 mark)**

42.

Explanation	True	False
A request is to ask for something.	✓	
An indulgent is an invitation.		✓
A container is used to put things in.	✓	
A bleak morning is a dismal one.	✓	

(1 mark for all correct)

43. to laugh; to walk; to fly; to grow **(1 mark for all correct)**

44. I have not got any / I've not got any. **(1 mark)**

45.

Verb	Noun
agree	agreement
refer	referral / reference / referee
form	formation / formality
assist	assistant / assistance

(1 mark for all correct)

46. end **(1 mark)**

47. We should have stayed late at school tonight. **(1 mark)**

48. I was eating all my dinner. **(1 mark)**

49. Annie's mum worked at the school library. The apostrophe is used for possession to show that the mum belongs to Annie. **(1 mark for correct use of apostrophe and for correct explanation)**

50. were **(1 mark)**

Paper 2: Spelling

These are the correct spellings:

1. island
2. delicious
3. potatoes
4. promise
5. favourite
6. weight
7. various
8. adorable
9. opportunity
10. relevant
11. persuade
12. stomach
13. curiosity
14. awkward
15. vehicle
16. mourning
17. stationary
18. caffeine
19. transferred
20. accommodation

Spelling Test Administration

The instructions below are for the spelling tests.

Read the following instruction out to your child:

I am going to read 20 sentences to you. Each sentence has a word missing. Listen carefully to the missing word and fill this in the answer space, making sure that you spell it correctly.

I will read the word, then the word within a sentence, then repeat the word a third time.

You should now read the spellings three times, as given below. Leave at least a 12-second gap between spellings. At the end, read all the sentences again, giving your child the chance to make any changes they wish to their answers.

Set A English grammar, punctuation and spelling

Paper 2: spelling

Spelling 1: The word is **shoulder**.
Jai hurt his **shoulder** playing tennis with his friends.
The word is **shoulder**.

Spelling 2: The word is **weather**.
The **weather** forecast for today is mostly sunny and warm.
The word is **weather**.

Spelling 3: The word is **naughty**.
Our **naughty** little kitten had scratched the carpet.
The word is **naughty**.

Spelling 4: The word is **fruit**.
Mangoes, pineapples, kiwis and oranges are all types of **fruit**.
The word is **fruit**.

Spelling 5: The word is **treasure**.
We are going on a **treasure** hunt tomorrow.
The word is **treasure**.

Spelling 6: The word is **return**.
The new clothes didn't fit so I need to **return** them to the shop.
The word is **return**.

Spelling 7: The word is **country**.
My ambition is to play football for my **country**.
The word is **country**.

Spelling 8: The word is **supermarket**.
The **supermarket** was extremely busy this afternoon.
The word is **supermarket**.

Spelling 9: The word is **equipment**.
At break time, we play with the outdoor **equipment**.
The word is **equipment**.

Spelling 10: The word is **temperature**.
The **temperature** water boils at is 100 degrees Celsius.
The word is **temperature**.

Spelling 11: The word is **infectious**.
The doctor said the rash was highly **infectious**.
The word is **infectious**.

Spelling 12: The word is **competition**.
Sam won a **competition** he entered at school.
The word is **competition**.

Spelling 13: The word is **average**.
Jemima was an **average** height for her age.
The word is **average**.

Spelling 14: The word is **cereal**.
Our family eats **cereal** for breakfast.
The word is **cereal**.

Spelling 15: The word is **confident**.
The actress was very **confident** on the stage.
The word is **confident**.

Spelling 16: The word is **artificial**.
The flowers in the bathroom are **artificial**.
The word is **artificial**.

Spelling 17: The word is **changeable**.
The weather is very **changeable** today.
The word is **changeable**.

Spelling 18: The word is **draught**.
There is a **draught** coming from the large window.
The word is **draught**.

Spelling 19: The word is **immediately**.
The building must be evacuated **immediately** if the fire alarm rings.
The word is **immediately**.

Spelling 20: The word is **committee**.
The **committee** members all attended a meeting at the school last night.
The word is **committee**.

Set B English grammar, punctuation and spelling

Paper 2: spelling

Spelling 1: The word is **island**.
The **island** of Majorca is close to Spain.
The word is **island**.

Spelling 2: The word is **delicious**.
The chocolate cake was **delicious**.
The word is **delicious**.

Spelling 3: The word is **potatoes**.
Potatoes can be mashed, chipped, boiled or baked.
The word is **potatoes**.

Spelling 4: The word is **promise**.
A **promise** should never be broken!
The word is **promise**.

Spelling 5: The word is **favourite**.
My **favourite** sport is cricket.
The word is **favourite**.

Spelling 6: The word is **weight**.
The **weight** of the luggage is less than 15 kilograms.
The word is **weight**.

Spelling 7: The word is **various**.
Various teachers have told me I have a talent for drawing.
The word is **various**.

Spelling 8: The word is **adorable**.
The kittens are **adorable**.
The word is **adorable**.

Spelling 9: The word is **opportunity**.
Playing football for the school team is a great **opportunity**.
The word is **opportunity**.

Spelling 10: The word is **relevant**.
All the **relevant** information should be underlined.
The word is **relevant**.

Spelling 11: The word is **persuade**.
I am trying to **persuade** my mum to buy me some new boots.
The word is **persuade**.

Spelling 12: The word is **stomach**.
My **stomach** feels full after lunch.
The word is **stomach**.

Spelling 13: The word is **curiosity**.
Mata listened to the story with **curiosity**.
The word is **curiosity**.

Spelling 14: The word is **awkward**.
The first time we met was a little **awkward**.
The word is **awkward**.

Spelling 15: The word is **vehicle**.
Ned's **vehicle** was the fastest.
The word is **vehicle**.

Spelling 16: The word is **mourning**.
The whole family is in **mourning** for our pet.
The word is **mourning**.

Spelling 17: The word is **stationary**.
Because of the roadworks, the traffic was **stationary**.
The word is **stationary**.

Spelling 18: The word is **caffeine**.
Coffee and fizzy drinks usually contain **caffeine**.
The word is **caffeine**.

Spelling 19: The word is **transferred**.
The gymnasts **transferred** their weight across the bars.
The word is **transferred**.

Spelling 20: The word is **accommodation**.
We do not mind what type of **accommodation** we stay in on holiday.
The word is **accommodation**.